Math Analogies

Book 1

Building Problem-Solving Skills

Series Titles

Math Analogies

Beginning · Book 1 · Book 2

Written by

Linda Brumbaugh and Doug Brumbaugh

Graphic Design by

Karla Garrett · Annette Langenstein · Trisha Dreyer

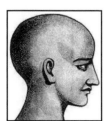

© 2009
THE CRITICAL THINKING CO.™
www.CriticalThinking.com
Phone: 800-458-4849 • Fax: 831-393-3277
P.O. Box 1610 • Seaside • CA 93955-1610
ISBN 978-1-60144-197-3

Mixed Sources
Product group from well-managed
forests and other controlled sources
www.fsc.org Cert no. SW-COC-002283
© 1996 Forest Stewardship Council

Teaching Suggestions

Analogies occur in life and frequently in high-stakes tests. Understanding analogies and the ability to reason analogically (reasoning used to identify, evaluate, and solve an analogy) are also important problem-solving skills. It is, therefore, beneficial for students to learn about analogies as soon as reasonably possible.

The immediate benefit is to recognize and solve simple analogies. The long-term benefits are improved reasoning skills that enable students to break problems into their component parts, recognize analogies imbedded in arguments, and evaluate them.

Problem-solving is an essential part of mathematical development. Analogies provide practice in breaking math problems down into their component parts, making it easier to recognize familiar formats that enable students to produce solutions.

Analogical reasoning is not easy, particularly for younger students whose thinking skills are in the formative stages of development. At this age, children commonly use guesswork instead of organized analysis to solve problems. For example, ask young children for two numbers between 10 and 15 and they will often guess or start counting from 1 to find the answer.

A challenge for young students learning to solve analogies is reading the format. For example, "A is to a as B is to" is not common language for a youngster. The interpretation skills mandate the realization that the phrase "is to" implies a connection between the item to the left and right of the phrase. Then, the word "as" relays the idea that there is a similar connection between the next two items, only one of which is provided.

On pages iv and v, we provide introductory lessons to help students read and understand analogies. We encourage teachers to work one-on-one with grades 2-3 students through this lesson and then monitor student work until it is clear the student grasps the meaning of an analogy.

We recommend that students draw and verbalize their answers. The drawing develops fine motor skills and the verbalization develops communication skills. Some young children may find drawing answers too challenging, but might be able to verbalize solutions. At this age, that is fine. However, these children should be encouraged to attempt to draw the solution after they verbalize it. Remember to keep learning fun.

The beauty of many of the items presented here is that they are language independent. Thus, non-native English-speaking students have the opportunity to participate with all other students in the challenges presented. When all students are involved, each one has the opportunity to learn the basics and beauty of logic and mathematics while developing and strengthening language skills.

The National Council of Teachers of Mathematics defined five content strands that should appear in the K-12 mathematics curriculum. These five strands are:

Number and Operations
Algebra
Geometry
Measurement
Data Analysis and Probability

The entries in this book are built around grade-appropriate standards for each of those five strands. While some of the analogies may appear too difficult or too easy for a student, there will be other related entries that should be suitable. If the analogies in this book become too easy for the student, try the next level, which is more challenging.

"Remember to keep learning fun."

Table of Contents

NCTM Standards (National Council of Teachers of Mathematics)

Number and Operations	1, 2, 7, 10, 11, 15, 16, 20, 22, 24, 28, 30, 33, 36, 38, 40, 43, 47, 51, 53, 55, 57, 59, 62, 65, 68, 70, 73, 75, 77, 80, 83, 86, 88, 90, 93, 95, 98, 100, 102, 104, 106, 108, 110, 112, 119, 127, 130, 132, 134, 137, 140, 142, 144, 147, 151
Algebra	3, 8, 12, 17, 21, 25, 29, 35, 39, 46, 48, 50, 52, 54, 58, 60, 66, 71, 76, 81, 84, 89, 94, 99, 105, 116, 120, 124, 126, 128, 131, 138, 141, 148
Geometry	4, 13, 26, 34, 42, 45, 49, 56, 61, 78, 91, 101, 107, 111, 113, 117, 121, 143, 146
Measurement	5, 9, 14, 18, 23, 27, 31, 37, 41, 44, 63, 67, 69, 72, 74, 79, 85, 92, 96, 103, 114, 118, 122, 125, 133, 136, 145, 150
Data Analysis and Probability	6, 19, 32, 64, 82, 87, 97, 109, 115, 123, 129, 135, 139, 149, 152

Math Analogy Sample Lessons

Teacher:

"The first girl is smiling. The second girl is frowning."

"To make these boys match the girls, what should the second boy look like?"

Teacher:

"This circle is white."

"This circle is black."

"To make the squares match the circles, what do we have to do to this square?"

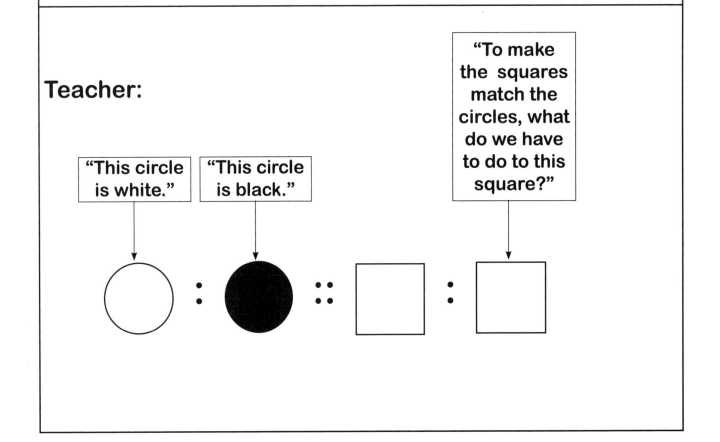

Teacher:

"This boy is pointing up."

"This boy is pointing down."

"To make the arrows match the boys, where should the next arrow point, up or down?"

  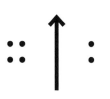

Teacher:

"The first girl is big. The second girl is small."

"To make the two circles match the two girls, what should the next circle look like?"

  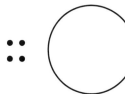

About the Authors

Linda S. Brumbaugh

I retired after teaching a total of 31 years in grades three, four, and five. Both my BS from the University of Florida and Masters from the University of Central Florida are in Elementary Education. As I look back over my teaching career, I enjoyed seeing the excitement on the children's faces as they encountered new concepts, worked with a manipulative, experienced some new mathematical application, or played a new mathematical game. It was stimulating when they solved an intricate problem, discovered something new to them, or got caught up in some new mathematical trick. As they got excited about learning, so did I. Each day of every year brought some new learning opportunity for me and for the children. I continue to work with pre-school and elementary-age children in the Sunday school system of our church. Our intent is to convey some of that excitement to each child who uses this book.

Douglas K. Brumbaugh

I taught close to 50 years before retiring after 35 years at the University of Central Florida. I taught in a variety of settings: college, in-service and almost daily in a K-12 setting. I received my BS from Adrian College and my Masters and Doctorate in Mathematics Education at the University of Georgia. Students change, classroom environments change, the curriculum changes, and I change. The thoughts and examples used here are based on my teaching experiences over the years. Our hope is that the thoughts in this book will spark the mathematical interest of each child who works with them.

Complete Each Math Analogy

1)

15 : fifteen :: 18 : *eighteen*

2)

greater than : > :: less than : <

3)

2, 4, 6 : 8, 10, 12 :: 14, 16, 18 : *20, 22, 24*

4)

square : ◇ :: rectangle : ▭

Complete Each Math Analogy

5)

 : miles :: 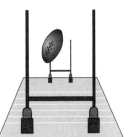 : yards

6)

 : $\frac{1}{4}$ :: 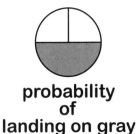 : $\frac{1}{2}$

probability of landing on gray   probability of landing on gray

7)

half : :: quarter :

8)

10 - = 6 : 4 :: 14 - △ = 5 : 9

Complete Each Math Analogy

9)

 : 12:05 ::  : 12:20

10)

10 tens : 100 :: 10 ones : 10

11)

6 + 9 = 15 : 15 - 9 = 6 :: 5 + 8 = 13 : 13-8=5

12)

10, 20 : 30, 40 :: 50, 60 : 70, 80

Complete Each Math Analogy

13)

 :  ::  :

14)

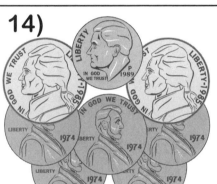 : **25¢** ::  : 100¢

15)

357 : **35** tens :: **246** : 24 tens

16)

half : :: fourth :

Complete Each Math Analogy

17)

 : **H** :: L :

18)

 : **quart** :: 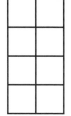 : 4 quarts

19)

$\frac{1}{6}$
probability
of
landing on gray
: 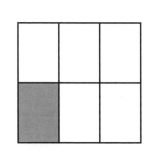 :: $\frac{1}{3}$
probability
of
landing on gray
: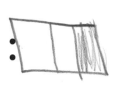

20)

$\frac{8}{8}$: 1 :: $\frac{3}{3}$: 1

Complete Each Math Analogy

21)

3 + 5 > : 7 :: 3 + 5 < : 9

22)

30 : 40 :: 31 : 41

23)

 : 41¢ ::  : 19¢

24)

6, 5, 4, 3 : 2 :: 19, 18, 17, 16 : 15

Complete Each Math Analogy

25)

26)

27)

28)

four hundreds
five tens   : 456 ::
six ones

six hundreds
nine tens   : 694
four ones

 # Complete Each Math Analogy

29)

357 : odd :: 246 : *even*

30)

31)

June 15th : Monday :: June 19th : *Friday*

32)

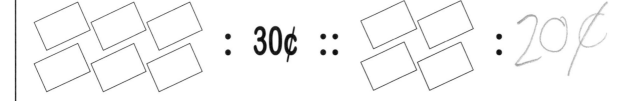

Complete Each Math Analogy

33)

> : **greater than** :: **<** : *lessthan*

34)

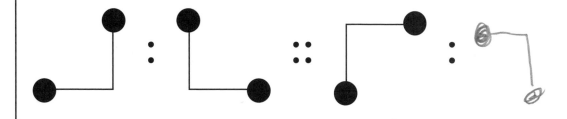

35)

1+1+1=3 : **2+2+2=6** :: **3+3+3=9** : *4+4+4=12*

36)

:: **eighth** :: : *third*

Complete Each Math Analogy

37)

 : 3:00 ::  : 3:30

38)

sum : add :: difference : subtract

39)

40)

 : **12** legs ::  : 16 legs

Complete Each Math Analogy

41)

$6.00 : $7.00 :: $9.00 : $10.00

42

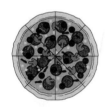 : round :: HOT PIZZA : square

43)

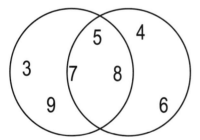 : **20** :: 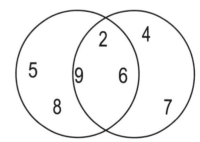 : 17

44)

$\frac{1}{2}$:  :: $\frac{1}{3}$:

dozen   dozen

Complete Each Math Analogy

45)

 : curved ::  : straight

46)

 :: 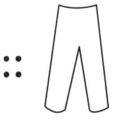 :

47)

130 : 140 :: 370 : 380

48)

Complete Each Math Analogy

49)

50)

odd : (399) 400 (401) :: even :

51)

addend : addition :: missing addend : subtraction

52)

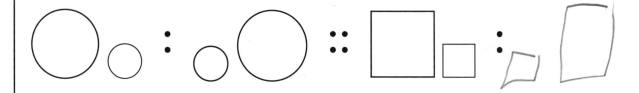

Complete Each Math Analogy

53)

465, 464, 463 : 462 :: 718, 717, 716 : *715*

54)

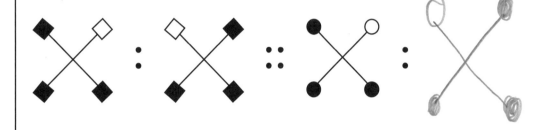

55)

38 + 49 : about 90 :: 31 + 42 : *about 70*

56)

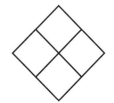 : 5 squares ::   : *5 triangles*

Complete Each Math Analogy

57)

 : $\dfrac{1}{4}$ :: : $\dfrac{1}{3}$

58)

 : **5** minutes ::  : 10 minutes

59)

$10 + 20 + 30$: **60** :: $11 + 21 + 31$: 63

60)

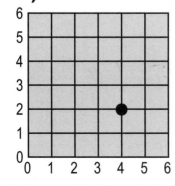 : **(4, 2)** :: 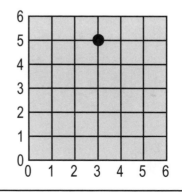 : (3, 5)

Complete Each Math Analogy

61)

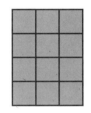 : **12** square units :: 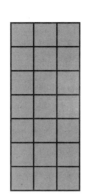 : 2¹ square units

62)

 :  ::  :

63)

1 week's allowance : **$2.50** :: **4** week's allowance : $10.00

64)

 probability of landing on gray : $\frac{1}{4}$ :: probability of landing on gray : $\frac{1}{2}$

Complete Each Math Analogy

65)

one thousand : **1,000** :: two thousand : *2,000*

66)

61, 64, 67, 70 : 73 :: 42, 46, 50, 54 : *58*

67)

7
years old
in
2009 : born in
2002 :: **4**
years old
in
2009 : *born in 2005*

68)

7,000 : 8,000 :: 4,000 : *5,000*

Complete Each Math Analogy

69)

 : 75¢ :: : $1.50

70)

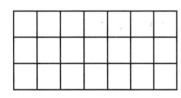

one half of a hundred : 50 :: one quarter of a hundred : 25

71)

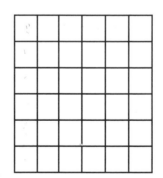 : 3 x 7 :: : 6x6

72)

1 minute : 60 seconds :: 1 hour : 60 minutes

Complete Each Math Analogy

73)

two thirds of **six** : 4 :: **one third** of **six** : 2

74)

 2 ounces : **1** gallon :: 6 ounces : 3 gallons

75)

$\frac{1}{3}$: $\frac{2}{3}$ :: $\frac{1}{5}$: $\frac{2}{5}$

76)

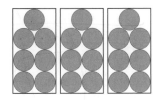 : 3 x 7 ::  : 5 x 5

Complete Each Math Analogy

77)

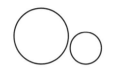 : 35¢ :: 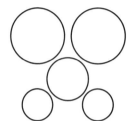 : 75

78)

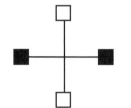 : 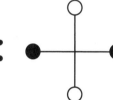 :: ⦿━━━⦿ : *of*

79)

MOVIE 🎥
Start Time: 1:00
Length: 1 1/2 hours

: 2:30 ::

MOVIE 🎥
Start Time: 3:15
Length: 2 hours

: 6:15

80)

9 **9** : 18 :: **7** **7** **7** : 21

Complete Each Math Analogy

81)

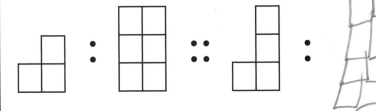

82)

 :  ::

83)

4 + 4 : 2 x 4 :: 7 + 7 + 7 : 7 X 3

84)

half of half :   :: half of whole :

Complete Each Math Analogy

85)

$\frac{1}{4}$: 25¢ :: $\frac{1}{2}$: 50¢

86)

9 x 0 : 0 :: 0 x 5 : 0

87)

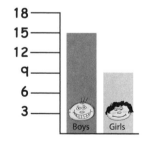 : boys > girls :: 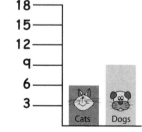 : cats < dogs

88)

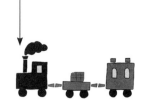 : end ::  : front

Complete Each Math Analogy

89)

3 x 3 : :: 2 x 4 :

90)

 : even ::  : *odd*

91)

half
square : :: half
triangle :

92)

 :  ::  :

 # Complete Each Math Analogy

93)

 : :: :

94)

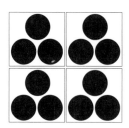 : 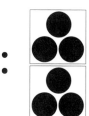 :: :

95)

30 : 40 :: 70 : *80*

96)

height : tall :: width : *wide*

Complete Each Math Analogy

97)

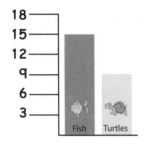 : fish > turtles :: 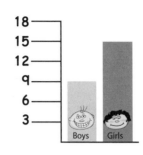 : Boys < Girls

98)

16 + 12 : even :: 9 + 26 : odd

99)

8 + 8 + 8 + 8 : 4 x 8 :: 4 + 4 + 4 + 4 + 4 + 4 + 4 : 7 x 4

100)

36 : six sixes :: 16 : 4x 4 48

Complete Each Math Analogy

101)

quarter
square
: :: quarter
circle
:

102)

24 + 32 : even :: 51 + 35 : *even*

103)

6:30 + 45 minutes : 7:15 :: 8:45 + 45 minutes : *9:25*

104)

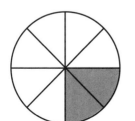 : $\frac{1}{4}$ :: 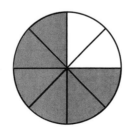 : $\frac{3}{4}$

Complete Each Math Analogy

105)

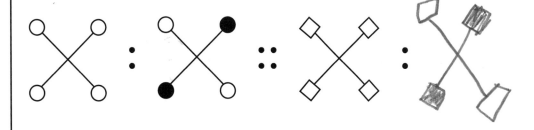

106)

$$3 + 3 + 3 + 3 \; : \; 4 \times 3 \; :: \; 7 + 7 + 7 + 7 + 7 \; : \; 5 \times 7$$

107)

symmetric :  :: not symmetric :

108)

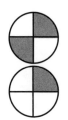 : 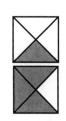 ::

Complete Each Math Analogy

109)

 : **12** ::  : 6

110)

I, II, III, IV : **1, 2, 3, 4** :: V, VI, VII, VIII, IX :

5, 6, 7, 8, 9

111)

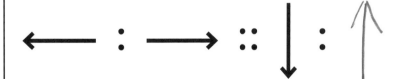

112)

 : **top** ::  : bottom

Complete Each Math Analogy

113)

8

: perimeter 32 units ::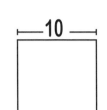
10

: perimeter 4e units

114)

 : 5 :: 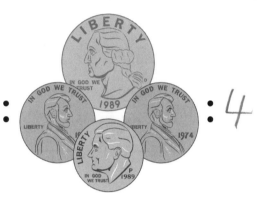 : 4

115)

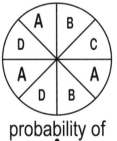
probability of **A**

: $\frac{3}{8}$ ::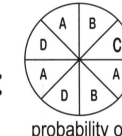
probability of **C**

: $\frac{1}{8}$

116)

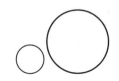 : :: 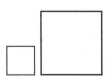 :

Complete Each Math Analogy

117)

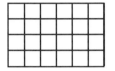 : area = 4 x 6 square units :: 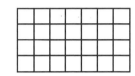 : area=4X7 squareunits

118)

$\frac{10}{100}$: dime :: $\frac{1}{100}$: penny

119)

69 : 96 :: 81 : 18

120)

 :  :: 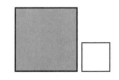 :

Complete Each Math Analogy

121)

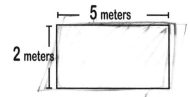 : perimeter of 14 meters :: 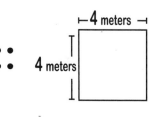 : perimeter of 16 meters

122)

1¢ : 1 :: 50¢ : 50

123)

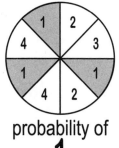 : $\frac{3}{8}$ :: 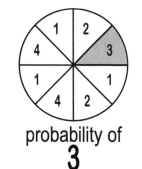 : $\frac{1}{8}$

probability of **1** 　　　　 probability of **3**

124)

 : 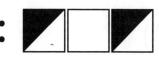 :: 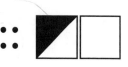 :

Complete Each Math Analogy

125)

November 18th : Wednesday :: November 22nd : Sunday

126)

 : :: :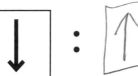

127)

500 : 50 tens :: 700 : 70 tens

128)

 :  ::  :

mouth

Complete Each Math Analogy

129)

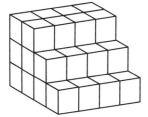 : 36 blocks :: 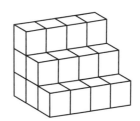 : 24 blocks

130)

15 + 10 : 10 + 15 :: 35 + 20 : 20 + 35

131)

TꞀ : TꞀT :: Ꭹ⅄ : ⅄⅄Y

132)

2 : 5 :: 7 : 10

Complete Each Math Analogy

133)

1¢ : $.01 :: 25¢ : $.25

134)

55 - 5 : 5 + 45 :: 80 - 20 : 5 + 65

135)

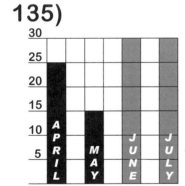

books read in April and May

: 40 books ::

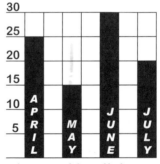

books read in all 4 months

: 90 books

136)

$\frac{1}{2}$ an hour : 30 minutes :: $\frac{1}{2}$ a half hour : 15 minutes

Complete Each Math Analogy

137)

V : 5 :: IV : 6

138)

 :  ::  : [handwritten scribble]

139)

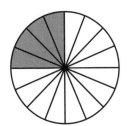 : $\frac{1}{4}$ :: 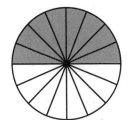 : $\frac{1}{2}$

140)

9 + 9 + 9 + 9 : 4 x 9 :: 8 + 8 + 8 + 8 + 8 : 5x8

Complete Each Math Analogy

141)

481 : 48 tens :: 761 : *76 tens*

142)

500,000 : 400,000 :: 300,000 : *200,000*

143)

  : 13
triangles :: 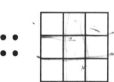 : *13 squares*

144)

  : 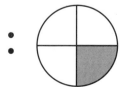 :: 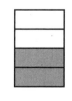 :

Complete Each Math Analogy

145)

 : perimeter 8 units :: 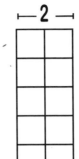 : perimeter 14 units

146)

147)

gray > white : 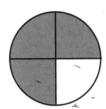 :: gray = white :

148)

335 : 235 :: 845 : 945

Complete Each Math Analogy

149)

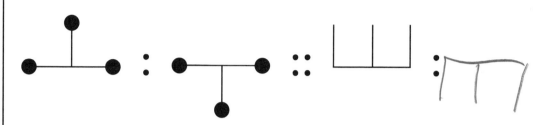

150)

 : area = 4 square units :: 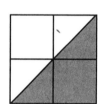 : area = 2 square units

151)

28 : 4 x 7 :: 15 : 3x5

152)

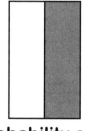 : $\frac{1}{2}$ :: 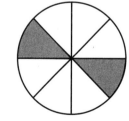 : $\frac{1}{4}$

probability of landing on gray   probability of landing on gray

Answers

Sample Lessons

iv)

iv)

v)

v)

(smaller circle)

Page 1

1) eighteen

2) <

3) 20, 22, 24

4)

(any rectangle is acceptable)

Page 2

5) yards

6) $\frac{1}{2}$ or $\frac{2}{4}$

7)

(any object with a single quarter shaded is acceptable)

8) 9

Page 3

9) 12:20

10) 10

11) 13 - 8 = 5

(13 - 5 = 8 is acceptable)

12) 70, 80

Page 4

13)

14) 100¢

(any dollar value is acceptable)

15) 24 tens

(4 is in the 10s place of 246, but there are 24 tens in 246. Think of money and you have 24 dimes and 6 pennies.)

16)

(any object with a fourth shaded is acceptable)

Page 5

17) L

18) gallon

(4 quarts is acceptable)

19)

(any object with a third shaded is acceptable)

20) 1

Page 6

21) 9

(any value ≧ 9 is acceptable)

22) 41

23) 19¢

24) 15

Page 7

25)

26)

27) 9¢

28) 694

Page 8

29) even

30)

(any 3 circles are acceptable)

31) Friday

32)   **20¢**

Page 9

33)   **less than**

34)

35)   **4 + 4 + 4 = 12**

36)   **third**

Page 10

37)   **3:30**

38)   **subtract**

39)

40)   **16 legs**

Page 11

41)   **$10.00**

42)   **square**

43)   **17**

44)

Page 12

45)   **straight**

46)

47)   **380**

48)

Page 13

49)

50)   399
      (400)
      401

51)   **subtraction**

52)

Page 14

53)   **715**

54)

55)   **about 70**

56)   **5 triangles**

Page 15

57) $\dfrac{1}{3}$

58)   **10 minutes**

59)   **63**

60)   **(3,5)**

Page 16

61)   **21**
      square units

62)

63)   **$10.00**

64) $\dfrac{1}{2}$ or $\dfrac{2}{4}$

Page 17

65)   **2,000**

66)   **58**

67)   **born in 2005**

68)   **5,000**

Page 18

69)   **150¢** or **$1.50**

70)   **25**

71)   **6 x 6**

72)   **60 minutes**

Page 19

73)   **2**

74)   **3 gallons**

75) $\frac{2}{5}$

76) 5 x 6

Page 20

77) 75¢

78)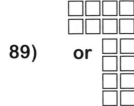

79) 5:15

80) 21

Page 21

81)

82)

83) 3 x 7

84)
(any half-shaded object
is acceptable)

Page 22

85) 50¢

86) 0

87) dogs > cats

88) front or beginning

Page 23

89) or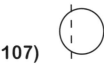

90) odd

91)

92)

Page 24

93)

94)

95) 80

96) wide

Page 25

97) girls > boys

98) odd

99) 7 x 4

100) four fours

Page 26

101)

102) even

103) 9:30

104) $\frac{3}{4}$

Page 27

105)

106) 5 x 7

107)
(any non-symmetric object
or symmetric object with an
incorrect line of symmetry)

108)

Page 28

109) 6

110) 5, 6, 7, 8, 9

111) ↑

112) bottom

Page 29

113) perimeter 40 units

114) 4

115) $\frac{1}{8}$

116) [square, square, larger square]

Page 30

117) area = 4 x 7 square units

118) penny

119) 18

120) [gray square, white square, gray square]

Page 31

121) perimeter of 16 meters

122) 50

123) $\frac{1}{8}$

124) [square with diagonal, lower-left shaded]

Page 32

125) Sunday

126) [square with left arrow]

127) 70 tens

(0 is in the 10s place of both 500 and 700, but there are 50 tens in 500 and 70 tens in 700. Think of money and you have 70 dimes and 0 pennies.)

128)

Page 33

129) 24 blocks

130) 20 + 35
(30 + 25 is acceptable)

131) YΛY

132) 10

Page 34

133) $.25

134) 20 + 40

135) 90 books

136) 15 minutes

Page 35

137) 4

138) [white, black, white, black, white bars]

139) $\frac{2}{4}$ or $\frac{1}{2}$

140) 5 x 8

Page 36

141) 76 tens

(6 is in the 10s place of 761, but there are 76 tens in 761. Think of money and you have 76 dimes and 1 penny.)

142) 200,000

143) 14 squares

144) [circle divided in quarters, bottom-left shaded]

(any half-shaded object is acceptable)

Page 37

145) perimeter 14 units

146) [arrows pointing up, left, down]

147) [circle divided in quarters, two left quarters shaded]

(any circle with only two-quarters shaded is acceptable)

148) 745

Page 38

149) [rectangle divided into two]

150) area = 2 square units

151) 3 x 5 or 5 x 3

152) $\frac{2}{8}$ or $\frac{1}{4}$